The Diary
of T. E. Lawrence

MCMXI

The Diary kept by
T. E. Lawrence
while travelling in Arabia
During 1911

Garnet Publishing

ISBN 1 873938 24 1

British Library Cataloguing-in-Publication
Data. A catalogue record for this book is
available from the British Library.

Typeset by Garnet Publishing Ltd.
Jacket design by Arthur op den Brouw.

Printed in Lebanon

Garnet Publishing Ltd,
8 Southern Court,
South Street,
Reading RG1 4QS, UK..

CONTENTS

INTRODUCTION

This diary was kept by T. E. Lawrence, then aged 22, when he undertook a month-long tramp through Northern Syria. It was not published until 1937, two years after his death, when the Corvinus fine-art press brought out 203 copies, of which only 150 were for sale. Although the material was reproduced in *Oriental Assembly*, it remains one of the least known of his works.

His family were living in Oxford when, in October 1907, Lawrence went up to Jesus College to study history. He specialized in mediaeval warfare, spending his summer vacations cycling around France looking at castles, many of which had been built about the time that the Crusaders were campaigning in Syria and the Holy Land. Lawrence became absorbed in the problem of techniques of fortification, and of who had invented them – had the Crusaders copied methods used by the Byzantines and Arabs, or had the ideas that they took out with them influenced styles there? He determined to go to the Levant to study the castles built before and after the Crusades.

Outside his formal studies Lawrence had taken a great interest in archaeology and had himself unearthed various artefacts, particularly pottery, which he had taken to show a family acquaintance, D. G. Hogarth who had just been appointed Keeper of the Ashmolean Museum. Hogarth had close contacts with the British Secret Service, then an ill-funded and rather informal organisation which had to rely for its information upon friends who could be encouraged to go shooting in the Caucasus or butterfly-hunting in Western China. Archaeologists, who could go to a place, move around, talk to the people, take photographs and make drawings without arousing suspicion, were of particular value and Hogarth had several times excavated sites of genuine scientific importance which happened to be near places in which the Secret Service was interested. During the War Hogarth was to head the Arab Bureau which processed intelligence about the area and several younger archaeologists whom he had recruited for his digs served on his staff. On the German side the redoubtable Baron Max von Oppenheim was operating in much the same way, and in the same area, while the scholarly Czech anthropologist Alols Xusil gathered intelligence about the Arabian tribes on behalf of Vienna.

Hogarth at first discouraged Lawrence's project of walking around Syria looking at castles, on the grounds that it would be difficult for a European to do so in the summer, and even arranged for him to see the explorer C. M. Doughty who confirmed this. Lawrence was not deterred and the Principal of his College asked Lord Curzon, the former Viceroy of India and future Foreign Secretary, to write to the Turkish authorities requesting letters of safe conduct for Lawrence which were duly granted.

Lawrence then spent July 1909 walking around

Palestine and the next two months in Syria, during
which he sketched and photographed 36 castles.
The following July his examiners regarded his thesis
on the castles as "brilliant" and awarded him First
Class Honours. He was still undecided about his
future, and considered taking a further degree with a
study of mediaeval pottery, or perhaps setting up a
press for fine printing with a friend.

During 1910 the Germans were constructing the
Baghdad Railway through Northern Syria, a project
which would enable German troops to approach the
frontiers of India without going through the British
controlled Suez Canal, and consequently was
followed with intense interest by British Intelligence.
Furthermore, on either side of the tracks the
Germans had been granted a strip, several
kilometres wide, which in Northern Mesopotamia
might contain oil. As the time for building a bridge
over the Euphrates approached, Hogarth obtained a
grant from the British Museum to excavate at
Carchemish, a city of the Hittites who had flourished
2,000 years before Christ: it was near the crossing
point over the River.

Hogarth used his influence with his own college,
Magdalen, to obtain for Lawrence the equivalent of a
Junior Research Fellowship which gave him £100 a
year, enough for him to work at Carchemish without
a salary. Before starting, Hogarth insisted that
Lawrence should spend two months at Byblos in an
intensive study of Arabic. On the site, where he

INTRODUCTION

arrived in February 1911, Lawrence proved a very good field archaeologist, in charge of recording pottery and of relations with the local staff, which gave him excellent reasons for finding out about their tribes and their relations with the Turkish authorities and with the other groups in an ethnicly mixed area of Arabs, Turks, Kurds and Armenians. He was also an expert photographer although it might be thought that his expensive telephoto equipment was more suitable for recording progress on the railway than in archaeological excavations. He established a close relationship with Ralph Fontana, the British Consul in Aleppo, who apparently co-ordinated Intelligence work in Northern Syria. He started to wear Arab dress.

The digging season ended in July, whereupon Lawrence started the solitary journey on foot that he recorded in this diary. One motive was to obtain further plans and photographs of castles so that he could expand his dissertation with a view to its future publication. It had not yet been decided whether finance would be made available for a second season at Carchemish and the area into which he went was little known: he might have hoped to come upon some new site for possible excavation, but probably also aimed to find out more about the people through whose territory the next stage of the railway had to pass. One of his letters to his mother showed that he was thinking of spending the entire winter in the area but after just over a fortnight he was struck down by dysentery so violent that he almost lost his life and had to return to England. He was, however, undiscouraged, and while there discussed with Doughty the possibility of wandering in the desert with the Sulayb, a nomadic tribe of hunters and tinkers. In July 1913 he was to bring the two people who looked after him during his illness, Dahoum and "the Hoja", the Carchemish foreman Muhammad Hammoudl, to England for a holiday.

In the meanwhile, Lawrence had two more seasons at Carchemish working with Leonard Woolley, another of Hogarth's protégés who, during the war, was to be involved in running agents into Syria. Early in 1914 the two of them, operating under the cover of the scholarly Palestine Exploration Fund, carried out a survey of Sinai which would be of great military significance in the event of war between Britain and Turkey. When it broke out he was in England but, early in December, he was called to work for Military Intelligence in Cairo. His speciality, until he was sent to Arabia, was, as is clear from his letters, Syria and the Baghdad Railway.

Robin Bidwell
1993

A note concerning the text of this diary

This diary was kept while the author was journeying through Northern Syria during 1911. It consists of notes jotted down whenever he had a moment to rest. As he travelled to most places on foot and was extremely ill the greater part of the time, the consistency of writing and spelling cannot be relied upon, especially as the original manuscript was kept in pencil in a small canvas-backed note-book and was never revised. The contradictions in spelling have been here transcribed as faithfully as deciphering will allow, without any corrections whatsoever. The introductory poem on the following page was written by the author's brother who was killed in active service while flying in France during 1915. .

To T. E. L.

February, 18th, 1914

I've talked with counsellors and lords
Whose words were as no blunted swords,
Watched two Emperors and five Kings,
And three who had men's worshippings,
Ridden with horsemen of the East
And sat with scholars at their feast,
Known some the masters of their hours
Some to whom years were as pressed flowers:
Still as I go this thought endures
No place too great to be made yours.

The Diary of T. E. Lawrence 1911

THE DIARY

The Diary of T. E. Lawrence 1911

On a Wednesday about July 12 I left Tell Ahmar and walked about an hour: then, feeling thirsty I went to some Kurdish tents, in which the villagers of some houses close by were staying, and got leben and barley bread; no money accepted.

Then walked on three hours till I came to the Khan, which was deserted: met a villager or two, however – one Shirlaub invited me to his tent. We had milk and barley pottage and bread, and then slept quite well: saw women grinding in hand-mill. Day hot: bright moon all night.

Next day, Thursday: Up before sunrise, and out before feeding, for Ras el Ain: 4 hours: stopped a little before and ate bread and leben in Kurdish tent: chief most hospitable: gave him a hejub to work at Tell Hamra if the English came: money refused. Went on to Ras el Ain ($\frac{1}{2}$ hr.) and stayed there $1\frac{1}{2}$ hrs. drinking and washing: a very pleasant spot and good water. In afternoon walked through liquorice and thick dust to Leruj. Took room at Khan and enquired fruitlessly about camera: met Nouri Effendi. Rice and Bahmia with bread. A little feverish.

Friday: Up and out for Urfa by carriage (1 med) after going $\frac{1}{4}$ to Khangi: slow drive:

saw nothing. Urfa about mid-day (7 hrs.). Took room in great Khan: then went out about 4 p.m. to photograph castle. Took it from the due west, showing the double gates and the line of walls from the πυργοκαστελλος to the extreme end. Warm, beautiful evening, with a little breeze. Rice and bahmia with bread, and was then kept awake half the night by a cheap theatre in the café over the street. Police asked for my papers.

Saturday: Up late (about 6 a.m.) and went out to the castle. Photographed the castle at the SE. angle: where the moat turns, and above which is one of the very few Crusader walls in existence here. It is patched in front (to R.) with Arab wall, but is very fine. A wide-angle photo. Then measured the E. side of the moat, and photographed the E. half of the S. side, by wide angle from the bottom of the moat. This makes complete my photographs of the moat, all but the north side. Then measured this E. half of the S. side and went and had some bread. Later I called on Gracie and had lunch with him: he mended my antinous release and my plummet. After lunch went back to the castle and measured till 5 p.m. Decided the N. side moat did not deserve a photo: average depth of moat about 40 feet. Greatest present depth 60 feet, but much filled in.

Crusade work is to be found in patches in the entrance gate-ways, at the SE. angle tower, and in a piece of the N. wall.

On coming down took a photo of the castle from a little street that runs NE. This view of the NE. angle of the castle and the back of the gate-towers looked pretty on account of the amount of green about.

In the Khan I found the chief of police and a follower, who remonstrated with me for going about alone. 'Boys might throw stones,' etc. He insists on a Zaptieh to-morrow. Would have slept excellently but for my wisdom tooth. This had me up two or three times. Drank some iced rose-leaf sherbet which quieted it.

Sunday: Up late (8 a.m.) and had a great wash; found police waiting for me all round the Khan; went up the castle with one little man. He complained of the heat, so I sat him under an arch with some snow and a bowl of water and tobacco, and he was happy.

Measured the interior, etc. A fresh morning with a cool west breeze. Took a photo of the interior of the castle from the tall beaked tower at the W. end: breeze rather troublesome, but could not get the tripod up: climb rather difficult. The angle tower is altogether Arabic.

Later on photographed the great gateway (also Arabic) from the top of a tower. Decided that almost everything in the place was Arabic except the moat, some straight pieces of wall, and the SW. angle tower: with the two Roman pillars.

Offered my little man (about 1 p.m. in the Khan) a ½-medjidi tip: he took it with thanks, but came back with it in half an hour, saying he was afraid the chief of police might hear.

Rested till three, then walked out to the vineyard and had tea and supper with the Gracey's: very kind both of them, but nothing new. Got back about 9 p.m.

Monday, July 17: Up about four, but was a long time getting on the road. The tooth rather worse: an abscess and face painfully one-sided. Bought a metallik of bread, and went over to the castle. Town wall is 9 to 10 feet thick.

About 6 started for Harran. No incidents, country everywhere as flat as possible; only huge tells about every two miles; crossed one small stream soon after mid-way. Much mirage: tried to photograph one pool, but failed: nothing shown on the ground-glass. The tower of Harran cathedral was in sight for four hours: all elongated by the mirage, it becked and bobbed in the most fantastic way, now shivering from top to bottom, now bowing to right or left, now a deep curtsey forward. Day very hot and drank five bottles of water between 6 and 2.30: did not stop anywhere on the way.

The people rough and unmannerly, half-Turkish spoken, and dressed in rags; children mostly naked. Many camels. Plain all wet and very fertile. Dhurra, liquorice, barley, and corn. No springs. Afternoon cloudy: was in shade for some moments. Soles of feet very tired. Camera case got very wetted, and back and hinge moulded all out of shape. Fortunately little damp leaked through, apparently.

Village people all called me 'sheikh'. Stopped outside Harran walls for a short rest, then climbed through a gap into the town. The main part of the village lay to the SE. of the old site, around the castle. Going there I met a Turkish captain, who spoke French wildly. He was leaving after regulating some recruit business with the Sheikh. I found the Sheikh in the castle, which he has made his house. There was a huge stone vaulted polygonal tower, with deep embrasures and an earth floor. In this he with seven or eight others was reclining, discussing the loss of a key. When I came in he greeted me, and called for rugs and cushions, and then I sat down. He was a young man, perhaps eighteen, with a sharp, rather rapacious and mobile a face, and dark curling hair: very broad and tall: of course thin. He had been sheikh only one year, since his father died.

We talked a variety of things (they were astonished that I was there so early from Urfa) and he rather strained my Arabic by asking for a description of English local government, and our marriage customs. He was also curious as to the dignity of Sheikh in England. His manners were excellent, very unlike the common people, for he did not snatch at my things, but waited (eagerly) for me to show them him.

Some of his men had heard of Jerabis (or Gerabis) as they said. They were interested in the coming of the railway.

At sundown he brought me food with his own hands: cucumbers, hard-boiled eggs, and excellent wheat-bread, while his men dined near us off boiled mulberries and bread. We had some of each. After dinner we talked a little, and then I went out to sleep. He brought me his best quilts, and I slept most perfectly, with his retainers in a heap around me. When I woke in the morning there was an old Turkey cock sitting on a low wall by my head, and many horses in the yard. I was lying on a low platform. Tuesday, July 18: Up by daybreak, and round the outside of the castle. The inside I had explored with the Sheikh the afternoon before. Feet very tired, tooth much worse. Side of face all sore and swollen.

The castle built at several periods: part of it quite late; none apparently pre-Arab: mostly of rusticated blocks: there was no ornament anywhere. Huge polygonal towers flank the other wall, and there is a sort of keep, of smooth stone, with shallow buttress-towers at the corners: inside this is vaulted on two square pillars in one room; others have plain barrel vaults. The castle has had a moat round it: perhaps a wet one. It has been a big strong place, but not over-interesting. The vaulting though is good. Then went and drank coffee (four cups) with the Sheikh and his men: about 30 or 40 at the drinking. They spoke uninterestingly. Later walked over to the mosque and looked for Miss Bell's column-capitals. Took a photo of a lion bas-relief in basalt – 5 ft. 2 in. long, 3 ft. 6 in. high, 1 ft. thick: broken in two pieces, rude work, muzzle broken, lying just outside the east angle of the town wall. A boy behind. Was found on the surface of the ground.

Then took a photo of the S. front of the

castle, not of the whole of it, but of the eastern half: this showed one small polygonal tower, and a line of walls, with the 'donjon' in the centre. Then walked round and took a photo of the great broken tower. Looking into it one could see the floors, and the central pier, and the rest of the works of the place. This tower stands on the W. side of the castle, defending one side looking towards the town. The former (S.) side looks towards the open desert.

Then went across again to the great mosque: could not turn over the other great capital, and found the little ones much damaged underneath, that is, the two I partially cleared. Not very interesting, these little ones.

Then started out seriously to take the Sheikh. Had taken him on horseback with his brother before the S. front of the castle, and now took him with a friend of his before the tower-room. Also took a photo of his brother, etc. Have promised to send him copies of these to Mr. Gracie at Urfa, for distribution. Gracie knows him, and his men come into the town every week.

Then we fed, about 9 a.m., on stewed mulberries, bread, cucumbers, and green stuff: very satisfactorily: wound up with grapes. Worked at the castle after lunch, measuring, etc.

Then walked across to Rebekah's well. I came in
past it yesterday, resting near it half an hour,
and the women as they came out to draw water
came and looked at me, singing. Some offered
me water from their wooden pails. The well is
down steps and very deep, cold, clean water.
There are camel troughs near it, possibly those
that Elijah used, for such things do not soon
wear out. Good water. Drank again to-day. They
call it Bir Yakub, and are very proud of it. It is
the only well outside the walls. I saw also the
Aleppo gate, a poor Arab thing, more
ornamental than defensive, in fact the walls of
Harran are slight defences: it is certainly not
fortified for a siege, with its long thin curtains,
and shallow towers, all square-angled. The
castle is the only fortress. There was a moat,
probably wet, all round the town, and between
it and the castle. There are no surface signs of
pre-Byzantine occupation.

The Sheikh is beginning to thaw out: he
called me his brother to-day, which is
condescension in a Moslem: but I increased his
prestige by holding a sort of levee in his livan in
the morning, and answering all questions of all
local gentry.

The great admiration of my little telephoto
tape has led to its disappearance. I went over

the castle again and decided it was all fairly late, post-Saladin at least, possibly post-Crusade. No more photographs needed. The great broken tower is about 60 feet high.

It appears from our evening talk that the Sheikh here is only deputy for his elder brother, whom the Government likes in Urfa. They are old régime and Ibrahim Pasha men, with 2,500 houses under them. This means a force of 10 to 12 thousand men.

A long talk on all subjects in the evening, especially politics: the Sheikh ended by going to sleep with his head on my knee! Ate off bread, grapes, and eggs: slept badly with tooth trouble and sand-flies.

Wednesday, July 19: Up about 4, and to the cafe for a time. Got the Sheikh to send if possible and find my telephoto tape: very unwilling, for he wanted me to stay over the day, or permanently in the village. Has offered me two first-class wives in his gift. The women here are extremely free, handling one's clothes, and putting their hands in one's pockets quite cheerfully. Also they never pass on without speaking.

Messenger came back without the tape: so Sheikh turned out himself, *et ne trouva rien dans le village.* Then he got on a horse and scoured the country: in about an hour he brought it back. All well! Found it with a Turk, who had taken it from my box while at Bir Yakub. Then we ate (9 a.m.) of eggs and boiled marrow and bread: after which I took a very ceremonious leave, amid earnest exhortations not to forget the photograph promised.

At 10.30 I was off, and went over flat country as far as Simbolat. At all villages I was most warmly entreated to stop: and at one which had a tell, and where I asked for seals, the women (who were alone in the village) forced me to enter a house and rest, asking innumerable questions, and giving me cups of water for drinking and washing. After half an hour I got up to go out, and was given a large handful of bread 'since it would be a shame to their houses if one departed empty'. These were Arabs.

After Simbolat (with Roman ruins) the road disappeared in a rocky hillside, so I had to take again to a compass traverse. By so doing, I reached Silaverik in a couple of hours, and passed it to 'Kilar Khass', some Kurd tents in a Roman foundation, where I spent the night. They were hospitable, but the women rude: all Arabic-spoken. I ate wheat boiled in leban, and slept on the new straw of the threshing floor.

Thursday, July 20: Up at four, after a perfect night, thanks to my Kurd host's abba, which kept out the straw most perfectly. Tooth much better; swelling going down: feet sore. Got off about 4.30 and passed over rough hills till 7.30. No water. At 7.30 found a Kurd village which spoke not a word of Arabic. Got bread and leben from them. Half an hour later came down into the plain of Serudj. I had then a very dull five hours' plod across the flat, until Serudj was reached about 3 p.m. I bought some bread and cheese, and then slept till about 7, after which I went out and saw Nouri Effendi, and then to sleep. The day had been cool and cloudy, with a shower of rain about 5 p.m.

Friday, July 21: Up about 4.30 after disturbed night: at first very hot, later very cold: no fever. Got off from Serudj about 5 a.m. with a pennyworth of bread. Ate half of it in the first hour's walk: in another hour was in the hills.

In the plain was interested these last two days to watch how the wind twists in spirals, often throwing up a thin column of dust many hundreds of feet. This would be done on an otherwise calm day. Walked over the hills for five hours, till I reached the first rivulet of the Euphrates valley: great joy: had a beautiful view from the head of the pass of the Bridjih plain. Stopped at the water for two hours; washed and cleaned up generally: the first clean water I had seen since Sunday.

Then about 1 p.m. got going again till 3.30, when stopped at Serudj Kopru. This is a bridge of two arches in limestone, across a green, swift rushing stream: from the sides of the valley just below the bridge come strong cold-water springs. Washed shirt II and wrote up the account.

Biridjih about 1½ hours away. Ate my other halfpennyworth of bread: feet very sore, but otherwise very pleased with the day. Then went on to Biridjih, and saw Basile, and appointed to see the carpenter next day: afterwards met the Khoja, and Yasim and Khalil Jadur in the suk: they very pleased to see me: all came and ate plums in my room in the up-town khan: about 9 p.m. sent them off. A very bad night owing to the multitude of sand-flies. They come perhaps from the trees opposite my windows.

Saturday, July 22: Up about 6; repaired feet with bandages (both festering!) and went off to see the carpenter. He says the Tcherkers bought the locks. Arranged with Basile about money if I stay the winter: saw the Kaimmakam and the Commandant about a zaptieh to come from Nizib with me; wrote letters to M., to P.G.; went over the castle, saw the Hoja, and Yasim with our boatman to Tell Hamra: also others from Jerablus. Afterwards bought two halfpenny-worth of bread and some plums: lay up in the Khan reading and sleeping until 4 p.m. Then went out to the top of the hill, and photographed the town walls, etc., from the S. The castle would be behind this hill a little to the L. Then went down into the valley and up hill again. Took the N. half of the castle from the NE. in the shade against the sun: and the S. half of the castle (both landward side) also from the NE. a little further on than the one before, and under the same disadvantage of light. This finished my films loaded. The next lot are meant for Rum Kalaat, K. el Nejru, and Aleppo. Tooth rather sore. Thereafter went to bed, first changing films in my room: slept better than last night, but very poorly: all sand-flies again.

Sunday, July 23: Feet better: up about 4, paid for khan and went down to ferry: bought two metalliks of bread, and ate it waiting for the boat: saw Shemali, who said there was now no work in all Jerablus: brought a message from Dahoun, to the effect that the Kala'at was sad.

Then set out from Biredjik for Belkis: road up

and down the cliffs. At Belkis nothing at all. Road continued Roman, in one place diving through the rock for a few yards. Road very pretty some hour or two after this: wound up a narrow and deep valley full of wood and fruit trees, to Shard'at, a pretty village where I had a row with the Mukhdar: he demanded a tezkereh from me, which I refused: he threatened to imprison me, and I turned and twisted him into knots. Ended by his kissing my hand in tears and promising never to be naughty again.

Went on another hour, to Krachtan, where made for house of Mukhdar: was well received, though a little shyly, for they are out of the track of travellers. Village is built in steps on the N. side of a narrow valley, running E. into the Euphrates, full of running water, and the wind-noise rustling up and down the trees. Like Blake's 'innumerable dance of leaves'. Thought a good deal of his *Jerusalem*, must have a copy sent out for the winter. Village all Turk-speaking, but an Arabic Taksildar and a Beyrout zaptieh, with two or three Arab-speaking people. Ate, about 6.30, of burghul and meat, with stewed apricots and beans, with poor bread. Then about 9 p.m., after coffee, they brought me a glorious white and purple quilt, and under that I slept till dawn.

Monday, July 24: Woke at dawn, to find the village stirring round my roof, which was being swept by a strong, cold gale, blowing down the gorge. Set off before 5 for Rum Kala'at. Feet better, tooth better. Road at first led through pistacio groves along the Euphrates bank. Trees like olives, but with leaves like a pear tree. Fruit grows in clusters, shaped like an olive, green at the stub, and growing from yellow to orange at the point. Size of small olives.

Road then left river, and climbed a sort of stair-way in the cliff, for an hour, to Djarmesly, a cave village in a cleft: then more climb, and almost at once a steep descent to the river banks opposite Khalfata, a village in Mesopotamia, with the house of the Kaimmakam of Rum Kala'at. Went along the river bank (bread and leben from a house) on a sandy path, with fruits and great water, and vines festooned among the trees overhead. This lasted an hour. Reached Rum Kala'at about 10 a.m. The place enormous, a town rather than a fortress. At first came part visible of a huge rock-moat, which cut off the peninsula on the S. (land) side; then the scarp of the Euphrates wall, about 60 to 90 feet of rock-cutting. I had then to walk up the side-stream valley to the gate of the place, before I could cross it on wide stepping-stones: a broad swift stream, shallow.

There was once a bridge. Walked round the far side of the little valley, half-way up. Took a general-view, wide-angle, showing the side stream, the hills, and the Euphrates. Another, a little farther on; another (ordinary lens) of the NE. valley scarp, in shadow mostly. This may be a little fogged. Then went on to the mouth of the valley and took one of the Euphrates front. This has a little domed building like a well in the foreground.

Felt sleepy, so went to cave, and slept till 2 p.m. Got up then, and (i) telephotographed the box-machicoulis of the NW. angle with a magnification of 13 and a stop of 22°: exposure 12 secs., on normal of $\frac{1}{50}$ nom f. 16. This was a large-scale photo of three machicoulis. Also (ii) telephotographed at $3\frac{1}{2}$ mags. L.P. all the range of machicoulis (c. 16) at f. 11 and an exposure of $\frac{1}{2}$ second. Both taken from the shade, and (i) with hood. These machicoulis very remarkable. More about them later.

Then went down into castle (down and up!). Through 5 gates, all double and protected by towers, one monolith with the outer-court. Then in shape of narrow ledge, running N. and S., gate to S. Builders of this place not satisfied with

90-feet wall and scarp, absolutely perpendicular, but put a rock-moat outside as well: moat once wide and deep: now all stuff of the walls and a graveyard have filled it up. The castle as a whole occupies the narrow point of a peninsula, a rocky ridge pointing due N. and S. This is surrounded on the E. by the Euphrates, on the W. by the little river Mezman Su, on the N. by the same: the S. end is thus the only part not precipitous. The crest of the ridge must be between 300 and 400 feet high. This is at the S. end, the highest, but not so high as the rock beyond the castle to the N. and S., from both of which it was overlooked, though at a fair distance off. The walls on the E. and W. run about half-way up the ridge and from inside them the rocks and ruins pile up, very steeply, to the central pinnacles. The highest point of all is very elaborately carved, and may have been a palace or a church. The locals say a minaret, which is probable afterwards, but all the ornament is not Arab. The building in the N. corner of the ridge-crest is a mosque, with paved court about it. Between this and the palace all is destroyed, except substructions and deep cellars cut in the rock. The view is limited, but tremendous.

The present village rests across the stream, on

the N. bank where it turns E. and W. and extends into the Euphrates. There are poplar trees, and the noise of water. The ridge at the S. end is about 30 feet broad at the top. This is cut down 90 feet to a path about 8 feet wide, like the razor in Westmoreland. The moat is about 60 feet wide. I took a photo of it from the Euphrates side, on a point of the castle about 30 feet above the edge of the razor. This is not satisfactory, but gives the river flowing at the bottom very nicely.

After this I left the castle (6 p.m.), very tired, but a most glorious place, and crossed the Mezman Su again by the crazy stepping-stones: the hardest I have ever walked over. I went to the little village (Kassala) to the Mukhdar's. He was away, but a kinsman and his son did the honours of the 'house'. They were living under a booth of fig-tree poles and oak-branches, and sleeping on top. We ate (about 7 p.m.) of bread, and wheat-leben porridge, and burghul boiled with pepper and pine-kernels. Then to sleep, about 8, fairly successfully, but not like last night, which was oblivion. Perhaps one does sleep better under purple and white silk coverlets!

Tuesday, July 25: Up at 3.45 (dawn) and had a wash in the stream, ate a cucumber, and had a lesson in bread-making from the women. By the way, not a man in the village knows a word of Arabic, so I am rather put to it. All pure Turk, which means very ugly, half-Chinese looking fellows with flat eyes and broad noses, and wide-split, tight-pulled lips of thin skin.

Wrote up this for a time and then stayed to eat, for there is no house but the cave-dwellers between this village and my night stopping-place. We had burghul and bread together. Then I went along the over river, west side path, till I could photograph the rock moat, and returned across the passage perilous, the stepping-stones that I know fairly well by now, to the castle. Feet not very good, tooth again too big for my head. Took a photo of the inside of the monolith tower, showing the applied vaulting. Tower about 17 feet wide inside between the inner jambs: the third gate counting from outside. The fourth gate, though also monolith, I did not think worth a photo, since it is only a single arch. The fifth is a very fine Arab double-arched gate. All this entrance-masonry is Arab and very good. The first two gates have machicoulis over them. Altogether one of the strongest and cleverest entrances in existence.

The Diary of T. E. Lawrence 1911

The manner in which the roadway is made to double on itself, so that it may be more easily under control, and the right-angled turns at most of the gateways are especially clever. There are no trap machicoulis in the floors, so far as these are preserved, and there were no portscullis. The box-machicoulis of the NW. angle are very small inside: only one tiny loophole in front, none to the side. A photograph was tried (under lighting difficulties) of the inside of the vault with which they communicate. There is another vault below this, to serve more loopholes. A photograph (w.a.) was also tried of the razor, looking almost directly down upon it. The lens was not wide enough to include all the moat, so the lower part is cut off. There should be enough all the same to make it fairly intelligible.

I made a few alterations in my Antinous. Then I looked at the mosque on the N. part of the ridge crest. It is quite plain with a date of ١٢٣٦ on a side-door. It is probably very late. The whole place is full of Arab ruins. There is only the foundation of Byzantine stuff anywhere remaining. I left the castle about 9 a.m. by a postern door in a tower on the river side, and walked to Khalfati. I noticed on the way that the people here use gourds, not skins, for swimming the Euphrates. This is here small and

and not as swift as it is later on in its course. Opposite Khalfati wrote up this account. Then climbed up my goat-track most laboriously, and afterwards came down the long shelf of broken rock-stairs, about 500 feet, into the Euphrates plain. Very tiring three hours' work. Pushed straight ahead fast through Enesh, Kachtin, and Shardak, to Belkis, a long walk of about 27 miles, with the goat-track thrown in. Feet a little sore, but no other damage. Average length of pace after first hour 2 ft. 7 in.; afterwards lengthened till in last hour 2 ft. 9½ in.

At Belkis made for house of sheikh, who was hospitable. Fed about 8 p.m. on burghul, shineneh, and bread. Slept extraordinarily well for the E.

Wednesday, July 26: Up about 4.30. Left about an hour later for Nizib. Road took me up hills at first, and then across a pleasant stream full of springs. After that through olive-yards and vineyards and fields of liquorice, to Nizib in about an hour and a half. There I bought two half-pennyworth of bread and the same of grapes, and went to the roof of a khan to eat them. Left about 10 a.m. after drinking an iced sherbet of distilled rose-leaves – a metallik of course – and went down to the bridge over the Nahr Kezim. I drank of this, and then went on to Kefr-Sheikh, the village of Ahmed Effendi, with whom I struck up an acquaintance last time I was out in Syria. I had previously decided not to take with me the zaptieh I had asked for from Beridjik. Feet to-day nearly right from the blister point of view, and fester on my hand also healed up. This shows there is plenty of reserve force to draw upon yet. On the other hand, my right instep has again collapsed. I suppose it will never get over the smash after my leg was broken. It is painful now in the morning, and after every rest, however short.

Ahmed Effendi received me with open arms, and gave me a sweetmeat of burghul and onions and spices, worked into a paste, and leben to wash it down. Not bad, barring the onions, of which I have smelt ever since. Then I looked over a history of Turkey with him (he is educated) and we went together to a spring and garden a few minutes from the house, and talked and drank all the afternoon. It seems he likes arrack! About sunset we came back to the house and sat and talked, he telling beads and smoking. Coffee appeared at times and sustained us till 8.30, when rice and chicken, with iced leben and bread turned up. After this we slept, I very well, till sun-rise.

Thursday, July 27: Up about 5 and after coffee and a piece of bread, on the road by 6. Walked 1½ hours to Yarym Tepe, where there is a great spring dammed up into a pond. Before leaving Kefr Sheikh I bought a little bronze horse found in the fields near-by (¼ med). Went on to Tell Basha, where I only stopped to glance at it, bigger than ever as it was, and turned off left at once for Tchflik, about four hours on the Jerablus road. Country all monotonous. Tried for seals in every village, but found nothing worth getting. Quantities of the more common sort. Prices extremely high in Bashar district. Left foot to-day altogether right; right very poor: abscess discharging all day. Bite on right hand begins to fester; left hand healed up – a matter of three weeks. Am now getting gradually into more 'Arabic' districts; nearly every one knows a few words here. But since Biredjik I have known more Arabic than any one else I have met: except one boy opposite Khalfati.

After 3 p.m. reached Tell Isau on the Aleppo – Biredjik road, very tired. Went on 1½ hours and missed my road in striking direct for Yasuf Bey. Finally slept at Nugluri, a little place with a 'tell' just before Tell Ker. Put up with the Sheikh, who was poor but hospitable, and had some ideas in his head. He was (e.g.) most forcible in

saying that every one should read: his child is
being taught. Fed about 7 p.m. on burghul,
bread, with iran. Chaffered about some antikas
and went to sleep.

Friday, July 28: First of Sha'ban: next month
Ramadan. Bought my two stones at dawn,
for 7½ piastres: found men, unwilling overnight,
waiting for me in the morning. One seal, round,
small, apparently two figures and sacred tree
between. The other an amulet in red stone (seal
in steatite) of the head of an animal: ox, cat,
sheep, horse, etc. They came with a small Hittite
pot of 'best' Carchemish period (watergate
house) from the village tell. Left Nughri about 5
a.m. and walked ¾ of an hour to a village with
a stone of a woman holding her breasts. Proved
to be a miserable Roman sepulchral relief. Went
on to Tell Ker, where ate bread and leben with
the village Effendi. Then to Hulman, and so to
Yusuf Beg, Tell Sha'ir, and the great spring in
the valley near Jerablus. This I reached about
12.30. Stayed till 4 p.m., washing, shaving,
repairing, and writing this. Then went on (1½
hours) to Jerablus. Anxious enquiries
everywhere if there would be more work, and
when the railway would come.

Reached Jerablus about 6 p.m., getting a huge

welcome from all parts. The women of the Hoja began to sweep and clean all the place as soon as they saw me over the hills. He himself rushed from the end of the village, and for an hour I held a levee of all the people in the village, and also of Mohammed Jasim, who came in from Kebilidji. Their greetings were something to hear. The Haji saptieh brought me two letters which Thompson had given him in Tell el Hamar. One from mother (June 23) and one from Mr. Hogarth a week later. Apparently a second season not impossible, which is the best news I have heard this long time. Very pleasant to have a change of clothes.

The Hoja filled me a special water-bottle of water, and gave me great honours and attentions. About 7 p.m. he brought in bread, and fried eggs, and khatir (yourt) and iran, and then (refusing to eat with me) went out and closed the door after him: this is the highest politeness I have ever met from an Arab. I was most exceedingly comfortable in his house with my big lamp burning and all things of mine about me, though I did not, of course, unpack my boxes of stores. About 10 p.m. I went on to the roof and slept, very soundly. Had a headache all the evening, but very pleasant to be with these men again. They are more mannerly than the other Arabs. The Hoja very anxious for me to live with him the winter. But the poor man is a most terrible bore conversationally, and sticks to one without end.

Saturday, July 29: Up in time to see the sun rise over the hills of Mesopotamia: very lovely in its colouring as this Carchemish plain always is. Sent off a man to Tell Halesh to the camel-driver to ask why the cement had not come. Found the camel-driver not at home, and no signs of any cement. So just started off for the Kalaat to measure the floor of the palace. Hoja started with me, but my distemper of the past few days increased suddenly, so I went on alone. Then it developed unexpectedly in a sharp attack of dysentery. I got on to the Kala'at into a lonely place and lay down on my back, from about 8 to 2.30, feeling most weak and ill. About 3 I sat up and tried to dress, but fainted promptly for about an hour, and again then when I made a second try. Under the circumstances I was afraid to go near the edge of the pit with the measuring tape, and so could not work. About 5 p.m. I got to the village, after a very hard walk. Decided to get out a tin of arrowroot, and send a man with letters to-night to bring a carriage from Biredjik. Cannot possibly continue tramp in this condition. Can hardly lift hand to write this. Dreamed when fainting of milk and soda! Sublime greeting from every man, woman, and child in the district I fancy, but I could not see half of them, so only did a poor best at politeness. Fed on arrowroot and milk about 6 p.m. To bed at 8 on the roof. Slept well.

Sunday, July 30: Spent the day in the Hoja's house, lying on my back. A good deal of internal trouble. Up about 4.30, fed about 6, on arrowroot and milk. Fainted again about 10 o'clock when a little way from the house, and cut my cheek rather badly on a stone. Rested so, with visitors to see me, till 6 p.m. when I fed, again of arrowroot. Dahoum came to see me. Slept about 9.30, badly. Up three or four times in the seven hours, and had headache besides.

Monday, July 31: Got up feeling rather wretched, naturally; fed about 8 a.m. No signs of a carriage or of my messenger from Biredjik. Hope he has not bolted with my money. The Hoja awfully good all these days with me making quite unprecedented demands on his time and patience. But poor man, a most dreadful bore as well, does his best by five or six repeats to get every idea of his into my thick head, which usually understands before he speaks. In the evening tried a little burghul well boiled in milk. Dahoum came to see me: slept about 9 p.m.

Tuesday, August 1: Up at sunrise after a fair night: dawn very glorious, with the broken blacks of the foreground leading to the silver line of the river, crossed by the rough points of the near poplar trees, and then the hills beyond, from deepest black at the water's edge, shaded to grey, purple, and finally a glorious orange, as the light caught them. Sunrise of course poor, as most sunrises are. Ate an egg in milk, and then went down to the river by slow stages, very painfully, and bathed. Needed a wash very badly indeed. River very low and frothy. Then lay on my back in the house till 4 p.m. when my man came back from Biredjik, without a carriage. The town doctor would not help him at all, and the Kaimmakam also refused. So now I must delay five days while I wire to Aleppo, or walk to Membidj. Will hope for Membidj: feel better to-day. In the evening again burghul and milk: Dahoum came to see me: slept about 9 p.m.

Wednesday, August 2: Woke up at dawn, which was like yesterday's: slept well on the whole: feel a little better. Ate an egg in milk about 8 a.m. then lay on my back and rested all day. Tcherkers agrees he bought the locks, but says the £3 were a present from Mr. Hogarth! Have written to Selim refusing to pay him anything. The Mukhtar has returned. Yasim wanted to marry, and so wanted money! Mended my things. In the late afternoon walked down to the Kala'at in one spell: – a great feat – and washed. In the evening chicken broth and burghul. Dahoum came. Slept about 9.30. Felt better all day.

Thursday, August 3: Woke at dawn after a good night feeling very much more alive. Will try for Membidj this evening. Fed about 9 a.m. on chicken broth and milk. Then opened my two boxes and took out slippers, etc., for use on board: have decided to go back to England. Packed also my Rabelais, Holy Grail, Rossetti, and Roland. At midday a little porridge. About 4 p.m. the bottom fell out of the Hoja's hospitality on a sudden. He refused me the loan of his horse, and tacitly refused the Membidj project. Proposed I should rest two or three days in Dahoum's house, and go by water to Tell el Ahmar. There being no boats I could not very well see my way to this, but I struggled down to Jerablus Tahtani, found a horse and hired it, and arranged to start in two hours' time for Tell el Ahmar with Dahoum. The boy was necessary for I have no small change with me, and if I cannot change a lira I cannot pay him. Returned at once to Jerablus Fokani and got into thicker clothes and finished my packing. We started about 6 p.m. The Hoja, very repentant, seeing me off. About 9 p.m. (marching with a fair moon) reached Sreisat, and slept two hours in the tents of one Mohammed el Kurdi: then started again, moonless, over difficult stony country, losing our way once, for the Euphrates. Reached this before dawn, but found access to the landing-place cut off by the Sadjur, broad, and deep and strong-flowing. Dahoum swam across to bring a boat to help me and the horse over. These two days, Thursday and Friday, thus run together.

Friday, August 4: The sun now rose. Certain people came to see me on the peninsula. They spoke a little Arabic. I feel fairly well this morning, most of the head-dizziness and inclination to faint gone. A boat came after an hour to the shore and I went to the Syrian bank. Then I gave Dahoum a medjidi and sent him off for Jerablus well content. I myself lay down in a hemp plantation till 11.30 sleeping and reading the Holy Graal. At 11.30 a waggon came across, and for want of a better I got on board and went with it very roughly and slowly to Membidj. Here I got eggs and fruit–salad with iced sherbet of lemons, sugared. Tried to arrange a carriage for Aleppo. Had a lot of trouble with various drivers, all asking thrice the fare, but eventually I found a 'victoria' going empty to Aleppo, the driver of which was glad to take a lira from me for the trip. It was now evening, and so I ate of a vegetable stew and bread, with iced sherbet of rose leaves for 4d. To bed about 8, in the khan: disturbed night.

Saturday, August 5: Up at three, and on the road a little later. Man has three horses, and so we went well upon the road. Some exceedingly rough stretches all the same. Reached Bab before 9 a.m. Pulled up at the Khan to wait out the mid-day. Ate a metallik each of bread and grapes. Feel less well than yesterday, but will soon recover this in Aleppo resting. About 2 p.m. went on and reached Aleppo about 7. Drove first to the consulate and recovered a bundle of letters, and then went to Barrow's. Fed and then slept most exceeding well.

Sunday, August 6: Up at 5 and read till 7. Then a cup of coffee. Not very well this morning. Wrote letters till dejeuner, and after it: also read a little. About 4 p.m. went out into the bazaar, and saw a little Jew dealer about Hittite seals. In evening fed and slept. Was better after midday, but very shaky all the time. Slept badly owing to excessive heat and the noise: a theatre just outside the house and two street fights with revolvers. Aleppo evidently not decadent in that respect. Police each time 15 minutes late!

Monday, August 7: Up about 4.30, read and wrote letters till 8. Then went out to see about money. Raised £10: saw the consul: settled up with him. Tried after embroidery. In the afternoon saw two antika dealers (one little red seal from one, two black and green from the other): also saw Haj Wahid. Then went with Tagir and looked out Thompson's map of Tell Ahmar. Saw Selim: tried the dealers for my lost camera: in the evening read till 8 p.m., when went out to the consul to dinner: much talk after till 12 p.m. Changed films on return to the hotel. Slept well.

Tuesday, August 7: Went out with Haj Wahid and searched the markets from 8 to 12.30 for embroideries: in end found two pieces that may do, for £4 Turkish: did not get more till these pieces approved. All embroideries made big on one size only, 6½ dhras by 1⅓ with a second piece 8 dhras by ¾. The pieces I bought are hand made: they are beginning to machine the stuffs.

Then went to consulate and saw Akras: back to hotel to lunch, very tired. In afternoon got out to Ottoman Bank: was ill on return, and lay down all the afternoon, dropping off occasionally in semi-faints. Wilkie Young came to see me. In evening felt a little better, and got down to dinner all right: there summed up enough irritation to tell my vis-a-vis he was a pig. Tremendous uproar of Levantines (little man a Greek Jew), 8 or 10 of them shrieking together and dancing about. I was the only person at the table who went on eating. Little man speechless with astonishment. Sudden irruption from near table of eleven mighty German railway engineers who told little man they had considered throwing him into the river which ran at the bottom of the garden, and would do it at once if he or his friends said another word. An immediate collapse of the Levantine element, which ate in whispers and melted silently away after the coffee. Landlord amusing, running and melted silently away after the coffee. Landlord amusing, running round the table during the row wringing his hands and calling aloud in Armenian. Slept exceedingly badly, high fever, great sweating and delirium. Worst night have ever had.

Wednesday, August 8: Got off 5 a.m. for station, 2nd class for Damascus, one only in carriage with me, so slept several hours: saw little en route: ate at Homs in new buffet. Haj Wahid saw me off at the station, and brought a huge water melon as a present: very delicious on the way. The قانون and I ate it together, and only finished it in the gates of Damascus. Reyak about 5 p.m., Damascus 10 p.m. Went to Palace Hotel. Slept well, though perspired a lot.

Thursday, August 9: Up at 7 a.m., breakfast, and sent for a haircutter: not very good, but quite clean. Afterwards looked over Suifi's stock, but saw nothing worth having. Ditto tiles in the Suk. Got the box with the hauberk I left here in Feb. and started for Beyrout about 1 p.m. Train overcrowded: very uncomfortable and high fever at Ez Zebedani: so went 1st where there was an empty carriage. Slept well there, and felt they went out at Aleih. Went on to Beyrout; a little feverish, sleeping much: reached German Hotel about 12 p.m., slept very well, though very hot, and perspiring.

Friday, August 10: Up about 7 a.m. breakfast, and then to Cook to take tickets to England: to Marseilles only finally: then to P.O. where letter from Will advising come home: to telegraph office to wire so to Mr. Jane: to Sarrafian about films: about 2.30 started by train for Jebail: reached it about 6 p.m.; feeling very well. Miss Holmes in great good-health: saw the new pottery and carried off a few samples: saw my boots, and a wauri's skin. Slept well.

Saturday, August 11: Left Miss Holmes about 2 p.m., got to Beyrout about 5, to hotel straight, and read a few papers, etc., till dinner: felt very tired and shaky, but must be getting better since I went up 20 steps at once without resting: to bed about 10 p.m.

Sunday, August 12: Up about 6 a.m. after a very bad night: high fever, etc., all the time. Cook came for my things before 7, and managed to get my box of antiques through the customs unopened! This was miraculous after the Jerusalem affair. Tipped him strongly. Boat very full of people, all Syrians apparently.

Left Beyrout about 11 a.m.

All over.

The Diary of T. E. Lawrence 1911

THREE LETTERS TO Mrs. LAWRENCE
WRITTEN DURING
THE AUTHOR'S JOURNEY IN SYRIA

The Diary of T. E. Lawrence 1911

CARCHEMISH

24 June 1911.

Have had orders to clear out as soon as possible: so in a fortnight we will shut down the digs. By the terms of the telegram from the British Museum they are so disappointed at our results that there will be no second season. It is a great pity for we had, on the strength of our former orders, just begun important clearances. We will leave the site like a warren, all disfigured with rubbish heaps and with all the work only half done: altogether about the most unsatisfactory job that one can imagine. So in a fortnight we will go down by boat to Tell Ahmar, and after three days there I will walk across to Harran, up to Urfa, to Biredjik, and back to Aleppo by Tell Bashar and this place. This will be a walk of about a month, for there will be several days each in Harran and Urfa.

I got letters June 1 and 8 yesterday: about June 1. Anxiety is absurd: if anything happens you will hear it by wire: I am well known in this district. The man-headed lion is in basalt, and as sharp as the day it was cut. The drawing was traced from a drawing on a camera ground-glass. Lots of our letters have gone astray, including Thompson's great report to [*Sir Frederic*] Kenyon: we now suspect one of the men who carried them to Biredjik. He would so save money on stamps. When away by myself I cannot write often because there are no post-offices. On this next tramp for instance there is only Urfa and Biredjik: and they are only two days apart, so I will only write from one. People seldom or never get ill out here: fever is not a serious ailment: it only at the worst involves resting half a day: small-pox I should be proof against, and typhoid is rare *in the country*: one is much more likely to get it in Aleppo, or even in Jebail. Neither Thompson nor myself has been in any way unwell.... Have found nothing for a fortnight, except some small scraps of Arab pottery, and a classical moulding. There are pots worse than the pebble-polished beauty; but all large scale work: much too big for white of egg, I'm afraid. It's two years since I lost that other camera: and it was at Seruj which is miles away. The Aleppo people knew nothing about it. The eloping Sheikh was the donkey boy's enemy: and the girl was quite willing to go: her relations (who are amongst our men) are very much distressed at the affair. For second cousins to marry is a terrible disgrace. The Sheikh is not back yet, but will probably be able to return soon, on a money composition. We did not get a photograph of the wedding: it was spread out on such a scale that it would have been hopeless. The donkey-boy mentioned above (Dahûm) is an interesting character: he can read a few words (the only man in the district except the liquorice-king) of Arabic, and altogether has more intelligence than the rank and file. He talks of going into Aleppo to school with the money he has made out of us. I will try and keep an eye on him, to see what happens. He would be better in the country, only for the hideous grind of the continual forced labour, and the low level of the village minds. Fortunately there is no foreign influence as yet in the district: if only you had seen the ruination caused by the French influence, and to a lesser degree by the American, you would never wish it extended. The perfectly hopeless vulgarity of the half-Europeanised Arab is appalling. Better a thousand times the Arab untouched. The foreigners come out here always to teach, whereas they had much better learn, for in everything but wits and knowledge the Arab is generally the better man of the two. I am not living in a tent: it is much too hot for that. I am

only sleeping on the top of the mound. The
river is swift, but quite pleasant for bathing: I
have been in a few times: but at present it is not
really warm (c. 90°). There are mosquitoes here
about the house in plenty: on the top of the
mound never, for the wind drives them off. I
have written to the Canon [*Canon Christopher,
of St Aldate's*].

I fear I will eat no beans from Oxford this year.
Will you get Will to add a copy of the Agonists
to my library, if he has read it, and approves.
Brazenhead must be procured in the Tauchnitz
from France. Glad you have joined the
Architectural. Prof. Petrie is always good. Prof.
Sayce is nearly 80 years old. You have been
wanting to go to Minster Lovel a long time. The
road to it after Witney is pretty. Many thanks for
boots etc. I expect I will be quite ready for them
when I reach Jebail. The report has been
delayed. It would be better if Haleb [*Aleppo*] was
made to slope forward a little حلب or حلب : but it
does not matter: it is entirely readable as it is.
ح this is h, the upright stroke is l and the ب is b:
vowels of course you have to guess. I will
winter either in Jebail or in one of the villages in
the plain here: the latter would be the more
interesting: and certainly as comfortable: an
empty fireless marble-lined hall does not add to

one's natural heat. If I can find someone here to teach me Arabic I will probably stay. We are such kings in the district that it would be a pity to spoil all our good work by abandoning it finally. It is quite extraordinary to see the difference our stay has made in the workmen. Will write as soon as I have settled this point. Petrie of course not needed now.

L.

TELL AHMAR

1911.

We have been here about four or five days working out a cuneiform inscription, photographing and squeezing things Hittite. Now it is all over, and to-day in the afternoon I am going off towards Urfa. The men here say it is best to go along the carriage road as far as Seruj (about 2 days) and then take another road. This route I may vary of course as I get later information. This village is one of the poorest, and quite the stupidest I have seen. Thompson will be carrying this letter in to Aleppo and will post it there, so you will get it quickly. After this you will not even expect another till I get to Urfa, in about a fortnight, from which to Aleppo is about a week in the post: so you see there is no hurry out here about that. Therefore allow three weeks after you get this letter and then if none comes allow another two days (Biredjik or Aintab). If that fails also it will be ten days *at least* before I write again from Aleppo; for I am going from Aintab or Tell Bashar back to Jerablus, to cement in place the pieces of a large basalt relief that I put together, but which is in the nature of things rather crazy. Thompson is sending out the cement from Aleppo, and our overseer, and the water-boy (the two men of brains) will do the work with me. Now about photographs. I have taken about 200 for the Museum with the three cameras I have used: of these all the quarter-plate of sculptures and some others are with my own camera. Thompson is going to ask Dr. Kenyon, the director of the British Museum, to let me have a set of proofs of these, since naturally I am interested in seeing them. If he consents (it is against custom) Thompson will either send them c/o Consul Aleppo, or to you. If they go to you, as I hope, you will recognise the parcel: open it, and look at the photographs yourselves, but *do not show them to anybody else on any account.* After you have looked at them send them out c/o Consul Aleppo or to Jebail if they come *within August.* If in September hold them to hear from me if I am coming back this winter or not. All the same the first week in September treat as August *that is address to Jebail* c/o Miss Holmes. By the middle of September you will know for certain if I am coming back or not. Will you ask Mr. Jane to find out for me if anything should bring me back to England this winter? I have written to him twice, but heaps and heaps of letters have gone astray: Did you ever get two large bundles of plans and drawings of Carchemish? I am anxious for you to see the photographs, for they will tell you all you want of the site: the book (which will come to you in 9 months time) will be interesting: but please remember to send out the prints to me afterwards, noting on the back any you would like me to preserve.

There are ten or 12 photographs of workmen: of these I hope two sets will be sent: the negatives are B.M. property: but the prints are Will's – his set and mine, and I will send accounts of the men represented: the young boy who is turning up his eyes horribly is Dahûm, the boy with whose father I may stay this winter: the boy can read and write, and so would be the best teacher of Arabic in the district.

The Diary of T. E. Lawrence 1911

JERABLUS

29 July 1911.

[*This was written when he was so ill with dysentery.*]

I am sending in a man from here to Biredjik tomorrow, so I will send a line to you. From Biredjik I went up to Rum Kalaat: from there to Nizib and thence to Tell Bashar and Jerablus. You will find most of these places in the map in my Thesis if that sorely battered book is still in peace. I have found nothing very new, nothing very good: the castle of Rum Kalaat yielded some new points, mostly Arab: it had a most enormous moat a perfectly appalling thing.... It cut off a mountain from a mountain along a col like the coupée at Sark. I am very well, and en route now for Aleppo. I got a letter from you here which Thompson sent up three weeks ago from Tell el Hamra. I am probably going now to stop wandering in Ramadan. I dare hardly ask for food from a Mohammedan house, and Christians are not common enough.

I have had the pleasant experience since a week of being the best Arabic scholar in all the villages I entered. In every single one, except Rum Kalaat, someone knew a little Arabic but I knew more than all: the people were all Turks and Kurds; a few Armenians and Yezidis. Rum Kalaat was my Northern point. This is nearly all I can write: the man is waiting anxiously – his own business, and I cannot delay him. I have the luxury of clean clothes, and am overhauling my stores. Thompson gave me free run of all the spare stores of the expedition, and as a result I am fitted out like the Swiss Family: only I have no embroidery silk or sugar mill.

L.

THE PHOTOGRAPHS

The Diary of T. E. Lawrence 1911

A note concerning the photos.

The photographs at the end of the volume were taken by the author during the time the diary was being written, and many of them are referred to in the text.

The Diary of T. E. Lawrence 1911

From Harran to Horum Kalasse,
the castle of Rum Kalaat

Sheik and his son, who was in
charge of the ruins of Harran

The Diary of T. E. Lawrence 1911

Close-up of Horum Kalasse
(built of mud brick),
with a view of the Euphrates

The Diary of T. E. Lawrence 1911

Bird's-eye view of Horum Kalasse

Sheik's two sons, blind Arab boy and villager

Traditional "Rebecca's Well", the only well
for miles in this district and upon which
the villagers of Harran depend.
About 1½ miles from ruined village

The Diary of T. E. Lawrence 1911

The base of the tower on the Harran Plain
which was once a Christian church,
later a mosque, now ruins

The Diary of T. E. Lawrence 1911

Kurdish village of Serug, or Sooroog,
east of the Harran Plain.
Mentioned in Genesis

One of the famous Hittite lions found in Serug,
but housed in the Urfa citadel

The Diary of T. E. Lawrence 1911

Urfa, from the Harran Plain.
Known as the "City of Abraham". Occupied by
Baldwin in the time of the crusades

Urfa from the vineyards,
showing the two famous towers

Urfa.
The main street to citadel and towers.
The channel in the middle is the
local method for sanitation

The Diary of T. E. Lawrence 1911

"Abraham's Pool", Urfa.
Once an Assyrian theological seminary, later
turned into a mosque, now largely a ruin